TIME

WITH GOD

THROUGH
PRAYERS, POEMS, SONGS
AND EXHORTATIONS

Gwendolyn Thomas

Copyright © 2016
By Gwendolyn Thomas
All rights Reserved

Library of Congress Cataloging – Publication data pending

Request for information, booking, and additional copies call Gwendolyn Thomas at (847) 907-1587 or email her at gwendolynthomas39@gmail.com.

Published by KAE DJ Publishing & Productions
12003 S. Pulaski Rd., Alsip, IL. 60803
Tel. (773) 233-2609

Printed in the United States of America. Unless otherwise noted, no part of this book may be reproduced in any form by any electronic or mechanical means, including information storage and retrieval systems, without permission in writing from the publisher except by a reviewer who may quote brief passages in a review.

Any references to real people, events, establishments, or locales are intended only to give this work a sense of reality and authenticity. Any character that happens to share the name of a person who is an acquaintance of the author, past or present, is purely coincidental and in no way intended to be an actual account involving that person.

Scriptures are taken from the King James Version of the Bible unless otherwise noted.

ISBN: 978-0-9904905-6-2

Contents

Foreword	7
Preface	9

Devotion
Daily Prayer	15
Guard My Heart	16
Throw out the Lifeline	17
Don't Look Back	18
Prayer	18

Encouragement
Let Go and Live	21
Look to God	21
Stand	22
In the Shadow of the Almighty	22
Through the Eyes of the Savior	23
The Seed	23
I Can do All things	24
Tomorrow Never Comes	25
God Shined the Light	26

Trust
Trust in God	29
Dare to Believe	30
Hope	30
The Holy Spirit	31
Praise	32
The Heavens Declare His Glory	32
Worthy	33
Universal Praise	33
My Help Comes from the Lord	34
We Shall Behold Him	34
The Holy of Holies	35
Savior Divine	36

Inward Reflections

The Word	39
Why Me?	39
What Do You See?	40
Purpose	40
He Holds the Reins	41
Searching for Love	41
The Heavens Declare His Glory	41
Caught Up to Meet Him	42

Worship

You Are My Being	47
Jesus Your Power Is Greater	47
Lord, We Are Waiting on You	49
Teach Me, Lord	50
Jesus	51
My Savior Is Coming	51
Jehovah	53
The Joy of the Lord Is My Strength	53
I Am Pressing On	54

Food for Thought

Prayer	57
The Contemplative Tradition:	59
The Holiness Tradition	61
The Charismatic Tradition	62
Hearing and knowing God's voice	64
The Voice of the Spirit	65
Keys to Hear From God	65
Psalm 27	67
Judah Must Go First!	68
References	71

In Loving Memory of

Pastor Lillian Pickens Stancill

Born into eternity February 17, 2012

Pastor Lillian Pickens Stancill was my spiritual mother in the gospel for thirty-three years. God revealed to her my spiritual potential and with his guidance, she endeavored to help me cultivate the gifts God had given me. The last memorable words by her to me were, "Stop second-guessing yourself, and use your gift."

Foreword

It is interesting how the things of God are so profound. When I reminisce on the heart of Gwendolyn, I'm reminded that her heart beats for God. In the simplicity of her character I find a depth that is priceless. Gwendolyn has accomplished what she would have thought an impossible task. She has put on paper her innermost thoughts and groans. They exemplify a testimony of her praise for every mountain God has brought her over. Knowing how she overcame the obstacles that life hurtled her way encourages us to know that God has the capacity to release us of our struggles and woes and that he can enable us to become overcomers. To understand the author through what has been written is to understand the book. I hope that these writings will lift you and release you to discover the one true and living God and to experience the gift of salvation that his sacrificial death brings.

Pastor K. Pickens
Trinity Full Gospel Church, Crete, Illinois

What a daughter! It is a blessing at age ninety to read my daughter's testimony. I am sure you will enjoy her thoughts as you read her poems, prayers, songs, and food for thought in *Time Alone With God*.

Lou E. Thomas
Mothers Ministry at Garden of Prayer Church in Broadview, Illinois.

Preface

Dear friends and likeminded believers:

God inspired me to write these poems and songs of the heart with the intention and hope that others would become free from the yokes of bondage which at times we all carry with us from childhood on into adulthood. These bondages sometimes cause us to never come into the fullness that God has predestined for us.

I stand amazed at the awesomeness of God's wonders. His grace for years has delivered me from oppression, depression, fear, and torment. Today I can truthfully attest that the peace of God dwells richly in my soul, so much so that I sometimes wonder how I allowed the enemy to torment me for so long. I am so thankful that God showed me I was not applying the kingdom power that Jesus entrusts to all who believe.

Luke 17:21 says, "For, behold, the kingdom of God is within you." When we have the kingdom of God residing in us, we should also have the assurance of knowing that the blood of Jesus Christ covers us. We have power over anything the enemy presents to us, because he gives us the power to reject it.

God's power existed in me, but I was not using it to the fullest capacity. In fact, I had become so accustomed to the demonic forces inhabiting my spirit that when the peace of God that passeth all understanding really entered in, I had to adjust all over again. You see, I had not known it, nor was I familiar with it. I had been dealing with demonic forces for so long that when God's peace entered in, it overwhelmed me. Praise God that I am no longer in my previous state of being and that this peace is free to all who believe.

You ask: How did this happen, especially since you are a Christian? First, we must understand that salvation is an ongoing process; and the deeper our relation gets in God, all those "tags" (that is what I like to call them) have to go. I was exposed to witchcraft as a child and as an adult, but I was not knowledgeable about it until God ordered my steps to Pastor Lillian Pickens Stancill. She had been a missionary in Haiti and had seen and prayed for many that were victims of witchcraft. I did not know how it could control the mind.

As a Christian in a leadership position, pride would not let me confess that I had a problem and needed help. Many of you today are carrying heavy burdens just as I was. You do not want anyone to know because you are a Christian or a Christian in leadership. As a leader, we must address denial, even if it exists in ourselves, because it can be detrimental to one's spiritual growth. Before healing can happen, we must first admit we have a problem and that we want to be healed.

This is where I was. I got tired of my condition, and I was so desperate. I prayed honestly and poured out my heart to God in desperation. I told the Lord I did not want to live another year with my life in the state that it was in. That is when God heard my sincere cry and healed me. What I love about God is that when he does something, it is well done. I knew something had transpired and something was going on in the spirit, but for the life of me I could not figure out what it was. Then one day God unveiled his Spirit of peace to me, and my life has been different ever since.

This can be you, as you read these poems and songs of the heart, seeking to find peace and crying for help. You too can ask God to unveil those things hidden within the depths of your soul that have tentacles, which do not want to release or allow you to be free.

I believe today, by the power of the Almighty God who we serve, many of you will never be the same after reading this book. Receive your healing and deliverance in the name of Jesus! After you have received your deliverance, do not stop there. Instead, share with others who are going through the same thing or something similar how you received your victory. As you become free, you will have the passion to help others become free of their yokes of bondage. I hate what happened to me, and I vowed not to let anyone I could help by the grace of God suffer as I did. As you continue to read, you will see how God turned my mourning into oils of joy, after God showered me with everlasting peace!

I give all praise to God for imparting words of inspiration by the Holy Spirit. I would like to thank Pastor Karen Pickens and the Trinity Full Gospel Church family for their support and encouragement. I thank my ninety-year-old mother, Lou E. Thomas. She instilled in me a strong will to never give up, and told me to keep persevering against all opposition. To my sisters and brothers Pauline, Vanessa, Harry, and Ervin: thank you for your love and support throughout the years. Lastly, to my children Orlando, Orlandus, Kristen, and Michaela: you are the greatest. You believed in me through my darkest hours and you displayed an amazing understanding of my dilemma when I became a single parent. I thank God that he helped you to understand that I was trying to raise you alone with God's help.

Sincerely,
Gwendolyn Thomas

Devotion

Daily Prayer

Lord, touch my heart,
That I may show compassion and understanding.

Lord, forgive sin,
So you will hear me when I call your name.

Lord, incline my ear,
That I may listen to your words of comfort, direction, and guidance.

Lord, word my mouth,
That I may speak your words and not mine.

Lord, open my eyes,
That I may see things as you do, and not the way I want.

Lord, direct my steps
In the path you want me to go.

Lord, as I follow,
Let me be captivated by the aroma of your sweet smell.

Lord, let me stand
In what appears to be the most adverse situation.

Lord, let me always portray
The likeness of you in my character.

Time Alone With God

Guard My Heart

Let it be so rooted and grounded in you
That nothing the enemy does can pierce it.

Lord, guard my heart,
That through it your love may shed abroad.

When words cannot speak the actions of my heart,
Lord, you will guard my heart,

That I may help guard someone else's heart as they go through the
fiery, piercing darts,

The trials and strongholds that are holding them hostage. As they try
to break free, Lord, guard my heart;

Keep it from being bound by the cares of this life,
That it may worship you and you alone forevermore.

Lord, guard my heart,

Engross it with peace that passeth all understanding,
and the wisdom to know right from wrong.

Gwendolyn Thomas

Devotion

Throw out the Lifeline

Lord, throw out the lifeline, for you promised you would never leave or forsake me. I feel as though I am sinking; gloom and despair have pitched their tent all around me. I am at such a low state I need you to throw out the lifeline.

Let your words that are written on the table of my heart revive my soul again. I long to hear your words of hope, faith, and all your promises that I read in your Word, your promises that will not return void.

Heavenly Father, please rejuvenate me and absorb my inner being until it drips like water from an overfilled sponge that cannot hold anything else.

My soul hungers and thirsts for you and you alone; no one can satisfy my spirit but you, Lord! Restore my will to overcome the cares of this life; and then let me count it all joy because you, my Father, overcame the world.

Lord, throw out the lifeline and feed my hungry soul; give me strength to press on toward the mark of the high calling.

Please give me wisdom to yield and keep an open communication, know my limitations, abide within my calling and reach for the lifeline when you cast it to me. Your lifeline captures and subdues everything that tries to attach where it does not belong.

Don't Look Back

Do not look back into Egypt at the things of old
that had you bound and entangled with yokes of bondage –
though life's journey seems to have
given you an unfair road to walk – or
was it because of choices we made
outside of the will of God.
In the midst of all this, God still shows mercy and intervenes; so instead of looking back and remembering all the bad things the enemy did to you, look at the good things that came through the trial.
Do not look back on all those painful incidents. Remember the good times and things that happened in your life.
Your healing waits for you now in the present.
Move forward past all those tags that want to keep you bound. Your healing is just around the corner.

Prayer

Prayer is the essential key that opens the windows to heaven's blessing.
Prayer will move mountains that seem impossible to climb.
Prayer turns a stony heart into a heart of flesh
And makes one's enemy your footstool.
Prayer brings peace in the midst of the storm.
It works when all else fails.
It prevails in your hour of distress and when you do not know what to say or do.
Prayer is the key to get to know God, and keeps your relationship with him new and rewarding!
It reveals the mysteries of heaven and revelatory things to you.
It will put your enemies to flight, it makes your journey easier to travel.
Prayer gives you faith and strength to believe.
You can endure and press toward the mark of the high calling.

Gwendolyn Thomas

Encouragement

Let Go and Live

Let go of the hurt and pain of life's misfortunes.
Perhaps because of negative choices or unknown circumstances you still hold on.
Let it go, so God can enter in and heal the wounds you
Have been carrying too long for things you cannot control.
Let it go, forgive, to be forgiven, and move on to brighter horizons.
Let go, surrender your will, and let the joy of the Lord have control.
Let it go, and do not look back, straight ahead, there is nothing behind.
Let it go, Gods wants to free you of old hurts and pain.
Let it go, and free yourself to do the work he has in store for you.
Let it go, so the peace of God can fill your soul.
Let it go, watch your life change, it will never be the same.
Let it go, and hold to God's unchanging hand.

Gwendolyn Thomas

Look to God

Look to God, who cares for you.
Look to him to lift your heavy burden.
Look to him to calm the raging seas and speak "peace, be still."
Look to him for the present and future, because the past is gone.
Moreover, we cannot change it.
Look to him from whence cometh your help.
Look to him when no one else seems to care or understand.
Look to him when things go wrong. He will be the light at the end of the tunnel.
When you look to God, things will not go wrong.
When you look to God, you are in the perfect plan and will of God.
Look to God who cares for you.

Gwendolyn Thomas

Stand

Stand when you feel you are all alone and there is no one but you.
Never compromise or leave opportunity for your stand in Christ to be questioned; it sends mixed signals.
By faith cling to the Word of God; through prayer and supplication make your requests known to God. Trust the Holy Spirit; he will empower to you hold on and fight the good fight of faith, run on and see what the end is going to be.
Never try to fight the battle yourself; let God take the reins and fight for you. "Put on the whole armor of God and the breastplate of righteousness, having your feet shod with the preparation of the gospel of peace." Be the one that Matthew 24:13 talks about and endure to the end.

Gwendolyn Thomas

In the Shadow of the Almighty

In the shadow of the Almighty I stand. Humbly I bow,
offering alms of thanksgiving and praise.
With outstretched arms and lifted up hands,
I give glory to whom it belongs.
For the miraculous things he has done,
Living in expectation of now faith
For the great things he is going to do.
In the shadow of the Almighty I stand.
I remember Gethsemane, the price that was paid.
Lest I forget.
In the shadow of the Almighty I stand,
Walking reverently, desiring to do his will.
In the shadow of the Almighty I stand.
Seeking to touch some lost soul and tell them,
Cast your cares on him who cares for you.
In the shadow of the Almighty I stand,
Finding peace that passeth all understanding.
It is my inheritance when I walk in the shadow of the Almighty.

Gwendolyn Thomas

Encouragement

Through the Eyes of the Savior

You can see the beauty of his love for you and me.
His eyes reveal a new creature in him.

We behold all things new, and see men as men and trees as trees. We are the redeemed and washed in the precious blood of the Lamb.

He restored our sight. We are no longer blinded by sin.
Now we see through the eyes of the one and only God.

Oh! How beautiful the new visions we see. We see brighter days ahead. There is glorious light shining bright at the end of the tunnel.

We see the sun shining through on a cloudy day.
We envision hope for the impossible, but most of all we see the portrait of love our Savior paints through creation.

I am so glad we can see, and someday he shall call our names!
In addition, our names are written in the Lamb's Book of Life.

I see angels praising our Savior in that faraway heavenly home
which one day shall be ours.

Gwendolyn Thomas

The Seed

Our life is just a seed planted here on earth to grow in the natural, but live in the spirit until we come into the newness of life, and realization of what our spiritual purpose is.

We may gather some thorns; they can be positive or negative.
If they are hindering our growth, they need to be removed.

Apostle Paul had a thorn in his side that was never removed.
However, it did not stop him from continuing to grow in God.

Imagine the rose; it was born with thorns, but they serve a different purpose – to protect. As long as it is kept pruned, it produces beautiful flowers.

Whether you have temporary thorns or permanent ones, do not let them deter you from fulfilling the purpose God has placed you here to do.

Be that seed that produces a plant and grows continually.

I Can do All things

I can do all things through Christ, which strengthens me.

There is no a mountain too high, nor valleys too low.

With God, all things are possible.

The sky is the limit; all I have to do is look to the hills from whence cometh my help.

When I find the path, I will in the affirmative walk therein.

I will hold my head up high and look to my Heavenly Father to guide my steps along the way.

I will walk out on faith and know that God is in my midst.

Knowing without doubt, I can do all things through Christ, which strengthens me.

Gwendolyn Thomas

Encouragement

Tomorrow Never Comes

Tomorrow never comes, but each day you see a new dawning is tomorrow.

As you walk in the path, God has destined every day to be that tomorrow.

When you look in the mirror and do not see the person you used to be, that is your tomorrow.

Yesterday you had a heart of stone, tomorrow has given you a heart of flesh in Jesus Christ.

Tomorrow gave you a new path to walk.

Tomorrow gave you a new song to sing.

Tomorrow gave you a mighty God to serve.

Tomorrow gave you a new way to walk.

Tomorrow has your new home in glory.

Gwendolyn Thomas

Time Alone With God

God Shined the Light

God shined the light within. The darkness that hid in the crevices of my heart, soul, and mind had to depart.

The powers of darkness cannot stand the light. I now can see the dawn of a new day beginning to shine in my life.

Each day as I walk in the newness of life, I am now free by the blood of the Lamb.

No more looking back into the clouds of darkness that overshadowed my soul; new mercies I see.

Truly, God has shined the light and I now bask in the presence of the Holy Spirit dwelling within.

Trust

Trust in God

When things are hard you cannot find your way.
Trust God – he never fails.

You wonder why opposition is a never-ending song in your life.
Trust God – he will not fail.

When sorrow compasses you all around,
Trust God to encamp his angels around you.

When your pain is insurmountable, his love will carry you through.
Let God heal your heart.

Life not going the way you planned? Don't give up; fight back.
Trust God to bring you out more than a conqueror.

His ways are not our ways.
Trust God; he knows what is best for us.

He is the Lord God that healeth thee.
Trust God in sickness.

When financial crises arise,
Trust God to be a provider.

Trust God to direct you into all truth and lean not to your own understanding; he will direct your path.

In all things, TRUST GOD.

Gwendolyn Thomas

Dare to Believe

Dare to believe that God can do anything but fail – that he is not slack concerning his promises.

Never stop hoping and believing in what you ask for in Jesus name!

You will receive as long as you ask according to his will. Dare to believe.

Seek the kingdom of heaven first and all things shall be added.

Dare to believe God will never leave you or forsake you.

If your ways are pleasing, dare to believe he will give you the desires of your heart.

He will give you joy unspeakable and make your life full of glory!

Hope

Hope thou in me is what my Father said to me.

I will make your life complete and give you joy everlasting.

Hope thou in me! You will never be the same.

Your burdens will be lighter and your journey much easier.
Hope thou in me! I am all that you need.

Only believe, grasp hold of faith, and walk into your destiny.
Hope thou in me!

I specialize in making the impossible possible. Hold your head up. Look to me.

I will never leave or forsake you.
Hope thou in me is what the Father says to all that believe.

Gwendolyn Thomas

The Holy Spirit

The comforter, which is God's gift to us, came to bring our lives to a new, rewarding level in him.

He will be our counselor when we don't know what to do, and the answer seems so far away!

A present help in times of trouble, strength when we are weak and the load is insurmountable.

He is our advocate and intercessor when we are at a loss for words.

He is always standing by, waiting for us to look to him for all our needs. Truly, he shall supply!

His blessings will make rich and bring no sorrows if you just trust and believe!

He and he alone can deliver when the yokes of bondage and strongholds of the enemy will not let go.

He will bring you out more than a conquer.
His riches you shall proclaim!

Let him in so he will rest, rule, and abide with you forevermore.

For he is the Holy Spirit!

Gwendolyn Thomas

Time Alone With God

Praise

Praise God in the highest, for he is worthy.
Praise God until the windows of heaven open.
Praise him with all your being.
Praise him to express your love for him.
Praise him until you become one with him.
Praise him for your victory.
Praise him for his Son and for his sacrifice on Calvary.
Praise him to confound the enemy.
Praise him for strength to endure all things.
Praise him when you do not feel like it.

Praise ushers in the presence of God and compels him to hear and answer.

Praise shackles the enemy.
Praise God for his blessings, seen and unseen.
Praise God to find peace and rest for the soul.
Praising never fails.
Praise God in honor and power.
Praise him in his glory and majesty!

Gwendolyn Thomas

The Heavens Declare His Glory

Morning by morning new mercies I see.
I lift my eyes to the heavens above.
The clouds array the sky
As the rays of sun shine through in crimson colors
Declaring the glory of the Lord.
Then suddenly he pulls back the curtain.
The sun bursts forth in opulent adoration.
It shines so bright; my carnal eyes cannot bear to gaze upon it.
For behold, it is a mini version of the radiance of glory shining through on creation.

The more the clouds move, the more I see him that neither slumbers nor sleeps.
Because they are the dust of his feet, each day we see a different veneer of the heavens painted and signed by the hand of God

Worthy

Lord, you are worthy of all the praise, of all the honor, oh so worthy. I lift my hands in reverence to your sovereignty.

Your power is awesome, mighty, and miraculous.

We bow down and adore you for who you are and what you have done.

Help us, dear Lord, to be more like you, and grant us your unconditional love.

Lord, we are lost without your direction.

You are worthy, O so worthy, of all the praise, and all the honor, oh so worthy!

In our hearts, we sing melodies of your majesty; it speaks peace to our souls.

When the stormy seas are raging within, you whisper "peace be still" and calm the sea.

Lord, let me be a living epistle of the sacrifice that you made; grant me the wisdom and grace to run this race with fear and admonition of your holiness.

Universal Praise

I arise to hear the birds singing their praise to the Lord God Almighty.
I look up and see the trees worshiping, waving their branches back and forth,

The leaves clapping in an awesome praise to the most high God.
The waves of the waters move back and forth from the shores, bowing in humble submission to God the creator of us all.
Through precept and example, God uses nature to show his people the importance of praise and worship.
We were created to praise God!
The universal praise is for all to be in one accord.
Lift our hands and heart, to praise and reverence the supreme God of the universe.

My Help Comes from the Lord

There comes a time when all doubt is removed and it becomes ever so clear where your help comes from.

There is no solution to the problem until we discover only the all-knowing Heavenly Father has the answer.

For he knows the problem before we are aware that one exists, and he has the solution before we ask.

He patiently and lovingly waits at the right hand of the Father to intercede on our behalf.

Oh! My soul, why do you carry such a load and burden of care?

Release it today into the loving care of the Master's hands, and forever be free from the enemies of the mind that bind the soul.

Christ's redemption on the cross demanded our freedom from the yokes that held us captive for years and those centuries before us.

We Shall Behold Him

We shall behold Christ our king arrayed in the beauty of his divine glory. There will be no need to attempt to explain what we see, because we too will be in our immortal bodies.

Our finite, mortal mind could not conceive the oblation that Christ made for all humanity.
Sweet, amazing grace! Our eyes are open, and we grasp the fullness of the revelation that began in creation and was predestined in heaven.

The Holy of Holies

Enter into the Holy of Holies.
Understand and realize that your heart, mind, and body must be surrendered to the will of God. There has to be a perfect submission to him.

As you arrive you will comprehend it is a place you have never been before. God has your utmost attention and you have his.

You are in a one-on-one session with the Master of all creation.

The commander in chief is speaking.

It is a place that you must diligently seek to obtain and cherish.

In it, you will get to know who God is, his plans and purpose for your life, and how much he loves you!

The Holy of Holies is a portion of heaven here on earth.
God is introducing us to the grandeur we will experience,
Oh but in a far greater way!

A place one wants to bask in forever. It brings peace, joy, and contentment to the soul that seeks to be satisfied.

As you leave this place, temporarily to return to the cares of this life, remember the Master has surrounded you and you are not the same.

You bid farewell for now, but the Savior shall return.

Savior Divine

He is amazing – so miraculous the mind cannot conceive the length, breadth, or height of his magnificence.

He is the Most High God, and no one can paint a picture or make creation like the Savior divine.

He speaks and nothing becomes something. The winds and waves obey his command.

He turned darkness into day, impregnated a woman to carry his Son, and cleanses to makes us whole again.

Tell death "not now" when the enemy tries to steal your life.
Wait patiently until death decides to surrender to God's will.
For he controls the universe and communicates to all the individuals in it.

For he never sleeps nor slumbers.

Inward Reflections

The Word

God's Word always has been and always will be.
All through life, we look for words of encouragement, accolades, and words to make us feel good about ourselves.
For the Word of God comes in its purest form. The Word is Jesus; the songwriter says, "He is the One."
Let us stop looking for words to validate us, but look to the "Word" to make us who we are.
Jesus, through his Word, made us righteous before his Father. He justified us through his blood, sanctifies us daily because it is an ongoing process, and when he comes again, he will glorify us.

Why Me?

I know you created me from the womb.

Your divine hand instilled something I could not see.

Why me, Lord?

I cannot do anything without your wisdom and knowledge.

Who am I that you would choose a wretch like me?

I have nothing to offer but a song of praise that you gave to me and a life that you paid the price for with your precious blood.

You are the potter and I am the clay.

Make me and mold me after thy own image.

You chose a vessel of dishonor to shape into one of honor to carry your holy Word.

You picked me up and transformed my heart and mind, to make me meet for the Master's use.

What Do You See?

Look into the mirror of your soul. Ask God to show you who you are and who he has created you to be for him in the kingdom of God.

You may not always like what you see, but grace and mercy always allow room for improvement.

View the picture you see in the mirror, as attire not quite appropriate. You need to change into a better outfit designed especially by God.

Your make-up needs to be refreshed, but God's grace is sufficient because he will make you look brand new.

Purpose

Everything that God created has a purpose:

To serve him and proclaim the good news of the gospel of Jesus Christ to all who are lost.

To speak words of encouragement and to feed hungry, lost souls. Spiritually and naturally, show them the joy of the Lord.

To share a smile filled with love and compassion.

To restore the hope and confidence in God and him alone. To serve others as Christ served us with his life.

To be like him.

To glorify God and fellowship with him by obeying him, keeping our eye on the goal of reaching heaven.

To know his purpose, we must have a relationship with the Father.

He Holds the Reins

God holds the reins to our hearts, souls, minds, and bodies. He is in control of everything. Surrender your all to him and move into your destiny. He holds the reins to your past, present, and future with him in eternity. Those things that seem impossible, he holds the reins. Surrender your all to God.

He makes your life complete.

He holds the reins to revelatory mysteries and reveals them to us.

Grow in his grace and seek him in diligent prayer.

Searching for Love

True love can only be found in the arms of the Savior.
He alone can love and forgive a multitude of sin, for his love is unconditional.

He sees in our heart what no one else can.

He provides us with different types of love when he creates us, but none can satisfy like the love of the Savior.

His love extends beyond our flaws and imperfections,
It builds character and integrity to glorify him.

His love, God's love is everlasting throughout eternity.
It is a love that only he possesses.

We strive to capture a portion of that love as our relationship with him increases.

The Heavens Declare His Glory

Morning by morning God declares his sovereignty in the heavens and clouds.

I lift my eyes to heaven above.

The clouds shroud the sky as the rays of sunshine shine through in crimson colors, declaring the glory of the Lord.

Then suddenly he pulls back the curtain.

The sun bursts forth in opulent adoration.

It shines so bright our carnal eyes cannot bear to gaze upon it.

The splendor of the rays shining so bright remind me of a mini version of God's glory shining through on creation.

As the clouds move, I see him that neither slumbers nor sleeps, because they are the dust of his feet.

Each day we see a different hue of the heavens painted and signed by the hand of God.

Caught Up to Meet Him

Caught up to meet God takes place in the twinkling of an eye.

Like a whirlwind of clouds going around and around, except you have no control.

This is not a roller coaster; you cannot get off when the ride stops.

Stay ready; this ride stops at the judgment seat of God.

There will not be any doubt in your mind, it is a heavenly tour only God can provide.

You will be caught up in the air to meet him; I know God showed me in a dream.

It is a wonderful experience if you are ready to meet the Supreme Being, our Savior and the Creator of all things.

Inward Reflections

One day humanity will be caught up to meet the all-knowing, all-seeing God of the universe.

Worship

When I no longer had words to speak, the Holy Spirit gave me words to sing. These are praise and worship songs inspired by God.

You Are My Being

I would be nothing without you; you are the air I breathe, the steps I take.

You are my voice of praise, and my song of melody.
Without you, I could not attain the impossible.

The joy you bring speaks peace to me.
It is my destiny to proclaim your liberty.

To hold the blood stained banner high and
Live a life of servitude.

The blood of the lamb has redeemed me.
Lord you are my being.

Without you, I would be nothing.
I could not see eternity.

Jesus Your Power Is Greater

Verse 1
Jesus your power is far greater, and transcends anything the enemy has.

It can move mountains and valleys, obstacles that hinder and stand in your way.

Your power is able to tear down walls and partitions, break down barriers that seem impossible.

Chorus
Lord, your power is greater than anything that I could ever imagine, Greater, so much greater, greater than anyone, greater than anything. Lord your power is greater.

Verse 2
You still cause the blind to see, the lame to walk, and the deaf to hear.

It keeps me in a world of turmoil, when it seems there is no way out.

When my soul is crying, "What do I do, which way do I go, what do I say?"

Chorus
Lord, your power is greater than anything that I could ever imagine, Greater, so much greater, greater than anyone, greater than anything. Lord your power is greater.

When the tempter comes to destroy and fill with doubt and fear. We search the whole world from coast to coast, all over the universe.

When there seems no hope, that is when we lift our hands to the heavens above, and pray to the hills from whence cometh our help.

Chorus
Lord, your power is greater than anything that I could ever imagine, Greater, so much greater, greater than anyone, greater than anything. Lord your power is greater.

I know now, Lord; there is no other way but to rely on the power. Lord, I put my trust in thee, because I know your power is able to keep me. Thank you for the power, praise you for the power.

Chorus
Lord your power is greater than anything that I could ever imagine, Greater, so much greater, greater than anyone, greater than anything. Lord your power is greater.

Worship

Lord, We Are Waiting on You

Lord, we are waiting; we are waiting to hear from you.
We need your mercy, Lord, your grace and power.
We need peace and love to shed abroad.
Please shower down your anointing, too.
We need to hear from you.

Lord, we are waiting. We are waiting to hear from you. We need your healing virtue.
We seek your Spirit to guide our steps.
We need your direction, Lord, to light our path.

Lord, we are waiting; we are waiting to hear from you.
We need to know your will.
Which way to go, O Lord!
How to walk, O Lord!
How to talk, O Lord!
Lord, we are waiting on you.

Lord, we are waiting; we are waiting to hear from you.
We know your way is right and we cannot go wrong when we hear from you.
We tarry here day and night, night and day in expectation.
Waiting to hear you speak.

Lord, we need you to breathe on us.
To refresh our souls to run this race and carry on. Strengthen us Lord to hold the blood-stained banner and raise it high forevermore.

Lord, we are waiting; we are waiting to hear from you.
Prepare us for each test and trial.
We implore you for wisdom, knowledge, and faith to continue.

Teach Me, Lord

Verse 1
Teach me, Lord, as I go from day to day. Teach me, Lord, as I walk in your amazing grace. Show me, Lord, which direction I should take as I travel this journey along the way. Guide my footsteps; keep me from going astray until I reach my heavenly home.

Chorus
Teach me, Lord, how to walk. Teach me, Lord, how to talk. Teach me, Lord, how to pray in a world that is filled with sin. Teach me, Lord, to praise my way through.

Verse 2
How can I thank you, Lord, for all that you have done? Show me how to live in reverence for all the grace and mercy you have shown. All I had was a life that was stained and marred. Then you showed your love and washed me whiter than snow.

Chorus
Teach me, Lord, how to walk. Teach me, Lord, how to talk. Teach me, Lord, how to pray in a world that is filled with sin. Teach me, Lord, to praise my way through.

Verse 3
Help me to walk upright before you, because you gave your only Son. No greater love has ever been shown. Teach me, Lord, to give that love to others as I walk this life for you. Lord, I present my life as a living sacrifice to you. I will serve you with my whole heart. All the glory belongs to you, and I will give you the praise you so deserve. You are worthy, worthy Lord.

Chorus
Teach me, Lord, how to walk. Teach me, Lord, how to talk. Teach me, Lord, how to pray in a world that is filled with sin. Teach me, Lord, to praise my way through.

Jesus

Verse 1
I serve this man; he gave his life for redemption of all. Oh what a love!
His name is Jesus, King of the Jews.
Do you serve him?
Do you worship him?
Do you praise him?

Chorus
Lord of lords,
King of kings,
Holy of holiest,
Righteous of righteous,
Bow down and praise him; lift your hands and give him glory.

Verse 2
Do you know whom you serve? Do you know whom you worship? Do you know whom you praise? Let me inform you: his name is Jesus, King of the Jews. Bow down and worship him, bow down and adore him, bow down and love him. Bow to the King of kings.

Chorus
Lord of lords,
King of kings,
Holy of holiest,
Righteous of righteous,
Bow down and praise him, lift your hands and give him glory.

My Savior Is Coming

Chorus
My Savior is coming; he is coming back for his church.
Without a spot or a blemish.
Will you be there?
My Savior is coming again, arrayed with his white-robed angels.
Dressed and adorned in majesty.

Will you be there?
My Savior is coming again.
Righteous and holy is he. He is worthy to be praised. Will you be there?

Verse 1
He is the King of Glory. His majesty reigns forever.
His wonders never cease to amaze me.
He is powerful. He is mighty. And God, you are so wonderful.
I would be lost without you; you said you would never leave me or forsake me.
I need your direction, Lord, your continued grace and mercy. Forgive me, Lord, for not yielding sooner in my life; but thank you for accepting me. Thank you for covering me when I did not deserve to be.

Chorus
My Savior is coming; He is coming back for his church.
Without a spot or a blemish.
Will you be there?
My Savior is coming again, arrayed with his white-robed angels.
Dressed and adorned in majesty.
Will you be there?
My Savior is coming again.
Righteous and holy is he. He is worthy to be praised.
Will you be there?

Verse 2
I cannot praise you or thank you enough. I am indebted to you. Lord, you give me strength when I am weary and the mind to obey your command.
Direct me, Lord, to where you want me to go, what you want me to say, what you want me to do. Shower down your holy boldness on me.

Chorus
My Savior is coming; he is coming back for his church.
Without a spot or a blemish.
Will you be there?
My Savior is coming again, arrayed with his white-robed angels.

Worship

Dressed and adorned in majesty.
Will you be there?
My Savior is coming again. Righteous and holy is he. He is worthy to be praised. Will you be there?

Jehovah

Verse
I love to praise you from the depths of my soul.
You give me hope to carry on, because I know who holds creation in his hands.
You have the power to calm the storm and raging seas and set free for eternity.
Hallelujah in the highest, you are Jehovah! Oh how I love you!

Chorus
His name is Jehovah. He reigns in majesty,
He rules the universe and all creation.
There is no one greater, no one wiser.
No one above, no one beyond.
You are Jehovah. You reign in majesty.
You rule the universe.
You rule all creation.
You are eternity.
Lord, we thank you for who you are.
Jehovah! You are forever; you reign higher ... than any mountain, wider ... than any ocean, deeper ... than any valley ... greater than anyone.
Hallelujah in the highest, you are Jehovah! Lord, I love you! O Jehovah!

The Joy of the Lord Is My Strength

The joy of the Lord is my strength will take you through and set you free.

It removes all doubt and fears within.

The joy of the Lord is my hope. Reach up and get it; it is there for you.

Release the cares of life today, so the joy of the Lord can enter in.

The joy of the Lord is what we need. Let go, let God have his way, and he will shower you with his joy today.

The joy of the Lord brings peace to sustain my soul. If it is love, peace, and hope that you need, he is waiting to supply you with his joy.

His blessing makes rich and brings no sorrow; it gives me faith to press on and believe all things are possible in him.

The joy of the Lord is my strength. It has brought me safe thus far, and I know it will take me all the way.

I Am Pressing On

I'm pressing on, gotta keep on pressing.
I'm pressing on, gotta keep on pressing.
I'm pressing on, gotta keep on pressing
On till I find my way.

Lord, lead me on.
Lord! Lead me on.
On through this land
Until I find my way.

Gotta keep on fighting.
I gotta keep on fighting!
Until I find my way.

I am moving,
I am moving on!
To higher ground.
Gotta keep on moving,
Until I find my way!

Food for Thought

Prayer

Prayer is an essential key in establishing a sound doctrinal foundation. In the spiritual formation of man, it was prayer that began to restore a fallen generation back to God. It enables one to live a virtuous life, one that is full of grace and operating in the capacity ordained by God. Prayer yields one to the will of spiritual gifts and enables the power of God to dictate and accomplish his plan and purpose for all individuals.

Consistent prayer keeps us in contact with God and builds a lifetime relationship with him. It helps us to grasp the character and image of God. The power of prayer strips off the behaviors of the old man and clothes the new man in righteousness and holiness. Prayer strengthens and equips the believer to a life empowered by the Spirit. A life filled with the Spirit brings about an action. It operates through the gift that God has instilled in people. Prayer heals, delivers, and sets free, then takes one to new levels in the Spirit.

Prayer delivers from the yokes of bondage that hinder individuals from reaching the heavenly vision that was predestined for them before the foundation of the world. Before we can go any further, let us define the origin and purpose of prayer. It is a two-way dialogue with the Lord, or simply having "a little talk with Jesus." The Bible tells us to "pray without ceasing" regarding the things that are on the heart, then expect to hear from God once prayer has gone forth without doubting. Always pray for personal troubles and the shortcomings you feel. A person should never feel that they do not have a need to pray. This is one of the greatest mistakes an individual makes. One becomes hard-hearted and insensitive of their inward being when there is a failure to pray. Foster and Smith said, "The Ten Commandments serve as a mirror and reflector of the soul" (p. 118).

They show people their weakness, perhaps not enough hope, love, or praise. These are things to put before God and petition for his help on. People must love God completely from the heart; ask him for help and continuously seek his mercy.

Prayer is the most powerful gift and tool to have.

Individuals should always go to God in prayer. When one goes to God in prayer whole-heartedly and honestly, God will answer if they wait on him. Alexander and Rosner inform readers that "prayer in the Bible addresses the personal God who reveals himself to human beings, created in his image" (p. 691). This resulted because of the fall of man, which created a breach in communion with God, and his unconditional love for a people he created and should be glorified. He instituted a plan to restore man back into communion with him. God promised (Gen. 3:15) he would give his son to bear the wounds of deliverance to all. That Jesus would be and is the one that is constantly interceding in prayer to God the Father daily for all believers. Although prayer was not active, God made the promise of prayer; it would come through Jesus the intercessor and redeemer for all humankind.

After the fall of Adam and Eve, God promised one to intercede. When Cain murdered Abel, God permitted prayer or worship to return to his people. This happened through the line of Seth. Man began to "call on the name of the Lord" (Gen. 4:26). Prayer was how the people communicated with God in the Old Testament, and it still exists and is prevalent today in the New Testament. Trent C. Butler affirms, "Israel is a nation born of prayer. Abraham heard God's call in the Old Testament (Gen. 12:1-3). In the New Testament, Jesus gave examples and teaching to inspire prayer" (p. 1320). Not only did Jesus inspire, he taught Christians how to pray in Matthew 6:9-13 and Luke 11:2-4.

Reflecting on spiritual formation entails a life guided by the ongoing work of the Holy Spirit engaging Christians to be more in the likeness and image of Christ. The manifestation of it embraces the process and practice of spiritual disciplines with a pure heart. We discover the "secret pathways" to God, and come to "know God rather than about God." Through prayer, fasting for spiritual transformation, seeking holiness, being Spirit-empowered, and serving in humility, Christians become whole and functional in a dysfunctional world. The Holy Spirit guides. God's plan is for man to be restored to the likeness and image of God.

Coming into the knowledge of Christ, we embark on a journey that our finite minds cannot begin to conceive or understand. We have no idea of what we are about to encounter. When we yield to the Holy Spirit and follow the paradigms of the holiness tradition, the contemplative tradition, and the charismatic tradition, the plan of God is fulfilled in our life. We will discover our "sacred pathway." Gary Thomas describes the way we relate to God and how we draw near to him (p.23). One can use the analogy of fueling up at a gas station; there are three different types of fuel. The higher the level, the better the quality and performance of the vehicle. Thus it is with the spiritual formation traditions and pathways – each transformation takes us into a better quality of spiritual life and engaging in the likeness and image of God. As we grow in relationship with God, the hunger and thirst for more of him increases. These traditions are founded on keeping a burning desire for our first love, a prayer-centered life in solitude, and the supremacy of peace, love, and joy of God. The power and love of God, not man, will provide a strong, simplistic, practical understanding of how we "grow in the grace and knowledge of our Lord and Savior Jesus Christ" (2 Pet. 3:18). We live in a world going against the will of God, and yet Christians must strive to remain wholly functional as the Holy Spirit leads. The key is to find the pathways that God has destined for us. Below we examine several of the traditions active in the transformation of Christians.

The Contemplative Tradition:

Richard J. Foster states: "A prayer-filled life is the steady gaze of the soul upon the God who loves us" (p. 23). Prayer increases one's trust in God and helps us to gain strength. The Bible repeatedly reminds readers of the importance of praying in faith. Prayer in faith creates a dependence to rely on God. He delights in his created beings trusting in him. This is a perfect illustration of the relationship between God the Creator and his creation. Through prayer, meditation, worship, and thanksgiving Christians express how they feel about God. Individuals should worship God in "spirit and truth."

The contemplative tradition focuses on the adoration, love, and supremacy of God and the attributes of his character that comes with it. The contemplative tradition is a life of loving attention to God. We should explore it, because through it we experience the divine rest that overcomes our separation.

Mediation and prayer work together in unity as we practice them in time alone with God. Reading the Scriptures daily a person can ponder and meditate on the Word.

Mediation leads to prayer. It creates time to have a conversation with God. Pondering God's Word in the heart directs a person to reflect on inward character. The Holy Spirit then reveals and equips us with words to express to God the things that are of innermost concern.

The two must connect because one prompts or empowers the other. Prayer helps to understand the Scripture that a person may have read during mediating. According to Donald S. Whitney, William Bates said, "Our desires are like an arrow shot by a weak bow. This is because we do not meditate before we pray" (p. 89). In other words, when we do not meditate, it may cause us to pray amiss and not be in the will of God.

The contemplative tradition constantly refreshes us in our first love and spirals our minds far above what the mind can conceive. Logical religious disciplines in prayer point out the privileged essence of our life with God.

On the other hand, the pitfalls, according to Richard Foster, are the tendencies to separate the contemplative tradition from one's ordinary life. Being obsessed with spiritual training is spiritual gluttony and is a failure to value intellectual efforts to articulate our faith. Love God with both the mind and the heart. These two must forever be inseparable twins. Neglecting the importance of the community of faith's stress upon our solitariness before God – a message we desperately need to hear – can lead us, especially in Western cultures, into an individualism that thinks only in terms of "God and me" (p. 23-58).

Consistent prayer and contemplating on the character and nature of God builds a lifelong relationship with him. Prayer bridges the gap to communicate with God. Practiced adoration of God through discipline establishes the spiritual formation of the contemplative life of Christians.

According to Butler, "Dialogue is what is essential to prayer. It makes a difference to what happens (James 4:2)" (p. 1322). One's ability to comprehend and perceive the concept of prayer, devotion, meditation, and worship ordains the power to discover and understand who God is. Coming into the knowledge of God and his supremacy clarifies that he wants to unconditionally respond to individuals. Loving God creates a relationship that is to be pursued and a desire for a more meaningful fellowship with God. It spirals one into worship and understanding the plan and purpose of God for those that seek him. It is accomplished through the work of the Spirit, and after much effectual fervent prayer.

The Holiness Tradition

Richard Foster informs us, "Holiness means the ability to do what needs to be done when it needs to be done. It means being 'response-able,' able to respond appropriately to the demands of life. The word *virtue (arête)* comes into our New Testament from a long history in Greek philosophical tradition, and it means simply to function well" (p. 82). To be holy is to be set apart from sin and draw near to God. Your conversation is motivated by God's perfect holiness; your conduct and behavior have been changed. To be holy includes obedience to what the Scripture says; and if we love God, we will keep his commandments. Love is the first and most important because it covers a multitude of sin.

According to Foster, "Holiness is not rules and regulations, other-worldliness, consuming asceticism, 'works righteousness.' Holiness is sustained attention to the heart, a bodily spirituality, 'a striving to enter in,' progress in purity and sanctity, and loving unity with God" (pgs.83-84). It is good to stay prostrate before God to keep the right concept of holiness and not become consumed with what it is not.

Continual prayer promotes holy living. It teaches one to live a virtuous life. Endeavoring to live holy establishes a virtuous life and transforms one morally. It compels individuals to make it a practical way of living. Through prayer, the process of life's fundamentals and characteristics are formed. Foster states, "The holiness tradition is a life that functions as it should. We should explore it, because through it we are transformed to live whole, functional lives in a dysfunctional world" (pp. 59-96).

Prayer and worship set up a standard of holiness for Christians to become accustomed to living according to heaven's way. They promote an effort of practice bringing the mind, body, and soul into subjection. It is an uphill journey, and one may stumble and fall. The key is to get up and start over again.

Individuals must develop a love that grows deeper as time progresses. Then the peace of God that "passes all understanding" enters in and the presence of God becomes evident. Then there is a delight in God that overshadows the soul. However, there will be moments of emptiness and darkness, because the soul begins to hunger and thirst for God in the midst of walking alone.

This spirals believers to a level that one's passion for God yearns to stay in his presence. God begins to clean all the negative things out, and suddenly one views things differently through the eyes and knowledge of God. Then a change comes over the heart, mind, and soul that directs our attention to God and his will for Christians to find rest in him.

Foster sums up the holiness tradition well by saying: "It constantly holds before us the ultimate goal of the Christian life: the goal of the Christian life is not simply to get us into heaven, but to get heaven into us! The holiness tradition has an intentional focus upon the heart, the wellspring of action. The holiness tradition gives us hope for genuine progress in character transformation" (pp. 59-96).

Prayer reflects the heart and is an outward affirmation, boldly striving to enter into righteousness through purity and a loving unity with God. God has given Christians the authority to live a virtuous life and to live holy, as they should in a sin sick world.

The virtuous and prayerful life enables one to surrender to the Spirit of God operating in and through people. Foster said, "Remember the threefold function of the Spirit: leadership, empowerment, and community-building" (pgs. 97-133). How should the Spirit function in one's life?

The Charismatic Tradition

"The Charismatic Tradition gives special attention to this other reality, which is, quite simply, life in and though the Spirit of God," according to Richard Foster (pgs. 97-133). The Christian life should be empowered by the Spirit daily, allowing the gifts of the Spirit to function actively in the capacity or area needed. Through the works of the Spirit, individuals are to be faithful biblical witnesses to build in love. One should not exemplify any efforts to stop the works of the Spirit. Any attempts to do so exhibit a failure to understand the purpose of the Spirit.

Foster also declares, "Tradition concerns itself with the relationship. There are key principles to prayer that contribute to having a victorious and Spirit-empowered life. One must always petition the throne of grace with humility, thanksgiving, and gratitude to God for his graciousness and many blessings. The charismatic tradition is empowered and directed by of the Spirit of God. Through the Spirit of God we are empowered to accomplish God's work, and it is living proof of his work on earth. We are to seek those who are empowered with wisdom. Always keep a teachable spirit, and God will direct your pathways."

Since God is working on us, transformations should be happening on a daily basis. We should be exhorting, encouraging, teaching, and instructing others in God's plan of spiritual formation for all. J. I. Packer clarifies, "Knowing about God to knowing of God, about relates to God, but knowing of God brings us into a relationship" (pg. 26). We realize this is an individual journey we are on, but we are to touch others while traveling along.

The objective is to take as many as are willing to go along, and try to be an example to those who do not seem interested. We then train the followers so they can take others on the journey with them, and the life cycle of spiritual formation continues. Paul said, "I beseech you therefore, brethren, by the mercies of God, that ye present your bodies a living sacrifice, holy, acceptable unto God, which is your reasonable service. And be not conformed to this world: but be ye transformed by the renewing of your mind, that ye may prove what is that good, and acceptable, and perfect, will of God" (Romans 12:1-2).

In the New Testament, Jesus gave examples and teachings to inspire prayer, and this is the center of all the traditions, along with the Word of God. Not only did Jesus inspire, he taught Christians how to pray in Matthew 6:9-13 and Luke 11:2-4. Therefore, we arch our spiritual formation on the foundation of prayer, engaging us into all the traditions via the Holy Spirit that makes us whole and ready to become citizens of heaven.

Prayer is necessary to live a victorious life filled and empowered by the anointing of the Holy Spirit. Practice prayer daily. We have victory, although the necessity to cope with the cares of the world still exists. Consistent prayer builds a lifelong relationship with God. The history of prayer has proven fundamental in establishing a sound doctrinal foundation. God ordained the promise of prayer that came through Jesus, the intercessor and redeemer for all humanity.

Prayer is the bridge that allows us to communicate with God. It is a practice and progress that eventually establishes the spiritual formation of Christians.

Hearing and knowing God's voice

All Christians hear from God (yes, God speaks to all of us). Oftentimes we do not recognize it because we have a tendency to look on the outside (looking for a word) instead of on the inside (through prayer). God will speak directly to you (Heb. 8:11).

Sometimes when we hear from God we do not know it or we do not give him the credit for speaking. Why? Because things clog our spirit. The enemy is dispatched to obstruct our hearing. Those of us who have an intimate communion with the Holy Spirit pose a big threat to his kingdom. Our goal is to tear the enemy's kingdom down.

Each of us are born with spiritual ears, but they have to be trained and disciplined to give heed to the Holy Spirit, or they will become dull of hearing (Heb. 5:11).

It is good to grow in the knowledge of the Word. Yes, we apply it daily, and write it on the tables of our hearts, but sometimes our spiritual man does not grow. The Holy Spirit gives us God's revelation concerning his will for us. When we pray and wait for an answer, through prophecy or through dreams, God can catch us quiet enough to speak to us. We do not grow until we begin to hear and of course obey (obedience is better than sacrifice, Deut. 8:3).

One fundamental truth that is overlooked and under-stressed is Christianity is more than a set of beliefs. It is also a personal covenant with God through Jesus Christ and the Holy Spirit as the CEO. Amen!

In the beginning, he spoke to Adam and Eve (Gen. 3:10). He spoke to Moses in Exodus 19:19. He spoke to Elisha in a still small voice (1 King 19:12) and the day will come when the dead will hear his voice. His voice will shake heaven and earth (John 5:25).

He is a life-giver; no one else can do this. The enemy is in competition with God to get our attention. Just like fast food places compete with each other, so it is within the spirit world. God is patiently waiting for us to draw closer to him and pay the price with praise and prayer. He is standing at the door knocking (Rev. 3:20). However, the enemy is busy trying to stop God from getting our attention.

Years ago, TV did not exist, and when it did arrive on the scene, there was only one in the house. Everybody watched it and turned it off at a certain time. I find myself guilty here. I am a movie watcher.

Then there is the DVD, CD players, and computers. The cell phone is at the top of the list. You would think we cannot live without them. People feel as though they cannot turn them off. What did we do before we had them? They are absorbing God's time.

The devil's job is to try to flood our being with noises that keep us from turning our focus on God. The kingdom of God functions one-way. Christians must live by every word that proceeds out of the mouth of God.

To live triumphantly and productively within the kingdom of God, we must listen.

The Voice of the Spirit

It is unbelievable that very few people know the voice of God/the Holy Spirit (Psalm 95: 7-8). Scripture states, "In the day that you hear my voice, harden not your heart." God is willing to speak, but people lack the ability to discern and recognize his voice. Learning to hear from God is one of the greatest abilities a Christian can possess. Jesus said, "My sheep know my voice, and I know them, and they follow me" (John 10:27).

Keys to Hear From God

1. One must have a divine desire. A true change comes when we find ourselves sick of our current state.

2. After a season of dryness, the Holy Spirit plunges us into a fresh dimension of himself (Matt. 5:6).

3. We must realize that we all have different callings. We should not try to be everything to all people. We need to abide within our calling in order to be effective for God (Eph. 4:16).
   - In 1 Tim. 4:7, Paul stated he had finished his course. We should not desire his course. We should strive to fulfill the course God has called us to. This is where we will experience the grace and fulfillment of God.

- Most importantly, live in a state of expectation; it will pull virtue from God. Remember the woman with the issue of blood: she was expecting to be healed once she touched the hem of Jesus garment. It put a demand on God. When you plug an electrical object into an outlet, you expect to get some power, so it is when you live in a state of expectation.

The gospel is not complicated. People complicate it (2 Cor. 11:3).

- Our heart and attitude should be trusting, childlike, and obedient.
- Sometimes we look for information and what we really need is revelation.
- God has taken the complicated issues of the world and composed the answers to all life's questions in the simplicity of the gospel (Heb. 8:11).
- God's answers are simple, not confusing. When an answer does not come easy or it is confusing, it is best to put it on the shelf rather than become more confused or make a mistake.

God never speaks in confusion or strife.
Example: Jesus took complicated problems like blindness, leprosy, and paralysis and simplified them into obedience, such as "Go wash," "Show yourself to the priest," "Take up your bed and walk" – philosophical yet simple.
The Holy Spirit ministers through revelation. In other words, it is unveiled.
To everything there is a cause and effect.
This is why Paul the apostle prayed this prayer (Eph. 1:17-18):

That the God of our Lord Jesus Christ, the Father of glory, may give unto you the spirit of wisdom and revelation in the knowledge of him: the eyes of your understanding being enlightened; that ye may know what is the hope of his calling, and what the riches of the glory of his inheritance in the saints.

Jesus rejoiced over this principle (Luke 10:21). The effect God promised to the pure in heart and motive (Isaiah 35:8).

One last key point: God talks to our Spirit.

Jesus said, "Out of our belly shall flow rivers of living water" (John 7:38). In the Old Testament God spoke through the priest by way of the Urim and Thummim. The Urim and Thummin were contained in a pouch, which was placed behind the breastplate, strategically close to the heart of the high priest (Exod. 28:30). The high priest kept the symbols for spirit and truth in his breastplate at all times. The spirit symbol Urim was for divine guidance, and the truth symbol Thummim stood for integrity of heart. We thank God for intelligent minds, but nothing exceeds the wisdom of God. We should endeavor to hear the voice of the Lord by making time in our day to be quiet before him. Pay attention to the Holy Spirit inside you. He will unlock any situation, answer any question, and solve all your problems. We must still ourselves before God and hear what "thus saith the Lord."

Psalm 27

David comes before God with a clean heart confessing his past transgressions. He acknowledges God is his salvation – meaning he believes and accepts God as the light of his life and the strength of his being. He is nothing without God, because he is illuminated by God's power. He places his confidence in God's covenant.

This particular psalm has two parts. Verses 1-6 are sung in a triumphant, heartfelt way. Verses 7-14 take a turn to a mournful, slow tune. We are to rejoice for heaven but mourn because some will be lost. He is happy for God's goodness, but sad for sin and its affects.

It emphasizes and shows that through salvation we come to the light; it comes through worshiping and reverencing God with a sincere heart. We cannot be doubtful and disobedient or unbelieving. The Bible says, "The fear of the Lord is the beginning of wisdom." We do not have to fear our enemies or the adversary because our trust is in the Lord and he will devour them.

His desire is to stay in the presence of the Lord, and to worship him in spirit and truth. It was David's ability to praise and worship with thanksgiving, then surrender wholeheartedly to God, which made him the apple of God's eye. He knew when he called on God "in the time of trouble," he would be there to make provision in the midst of his enemies. David was confident he was safe in the presence of God.

He prays to God to deliver him from trouble, forgive his sins, and protect from evil. He knew God's strength would sustain him when everyone else failed. He knows God is his covering and his protector. God will raise him up high above and shelter him from the enemies. This assurance is the reason he sacrifices praise regardless of his circumstances. He has learned how to encourage himself in the midst of trouble.

Verse seven takes a turn. Out of the depths of his heart and soul, David cries out to God as though he cannot bear any more trouble. He cries out to God for deliverance from the hands of the enemy. He knows his help can only come from the Lord – anyone else would not be sufficient. David comes before God with a clean heart, confessing his past transgression, stating he has not always been or done what is right, pleading with God not to hide his face from him nor be angry.

When my mother and father, the closest natural thing to me, forsakes me, Lord, I know you will be there. I am confident you will not leave me. He begins to take a stand and have faith.

After he has acknowledged God, entreated and praised him for who he is, his prayer turns again. Now that he knows he has his attention and he is listening, David then petitions God. He asks God for instruction and guidance because his enemies are within his palace and without. He needs God's divine protection.

David is now confident and reassured because he has been in the presence of the Lord and he knows he will not be overtaken. God's grace and mercy is revealed to him here on earth in the land of the living. He speaks things into existence by faith. He acknowledges that he is in the affirmative going to wait on God. He will be strong at heart. He renews his trust and hope in God. Then he makes a covenant with God to wait on him.

Judah Must Go First!

We are daily fighting a spiritual war against wickedness and principalities in high places. Before we enter into war, we must put on our war clothes and acknowledge our war cry. *Yadah* means praise in Hebrew; it is also the Hebrew word for Judah.

Anything we attempt to do, Judah must come first. We must praise and acknowledge God. Why? Because Judah accepted full responsibility for our life. Praise must go first. In Judges 1:1-12, Israel was preparing to go to battle and they asked the Lord: who will go first to lay down his life against the Canaanites? God said, "Judah is to go first."

In Judges 20:18 they asked who would be the first to go against the Benjamites. God said, "Judah is to go first." Before any battle, praise must go first. Why must Judah go first?

Leah, after bearing Jacob three sons, was still not his favorite, and she was hated by Rachel, her sister. When Leah had Judah, she said, "I'm going to praise God" (Gen. 29:35). She began to praise God, and Judah was blessed. God gave her lineage to the Messiah.

When Judah or praise goes first, the middle wall of partition is destroyed.

When Judah goes first, our battles and struggles become easier.

When Judah goes first, we declare the attributes of God.

When Judah goes first, we are saying: Lord, I am falling short of the standard. I need thee, the Lion of Judah, to fix me. Fight my battles, guide my footsteps, heal me, and deliver me.

When Judah goes first, I confess my faults and receive forgiveness for my sins and I am reconciled to God.

When Judah goes first, I can now have relationship with God. I can receive forgiveness and confess God's grace, his mercy, his love, and his victory. I can exalt his name and give thanks when Judah goes first.

When Judah goes first, the gates of hell shall not prevail against thee.

When Judah goes first, praise goes first. Closed doors will become open.

When Judah goes first, your broken heart is healed.

When Judah goes first, he will heal your sin sick soul.

Praise opens the door to the Lion of Judah. The Lion of Judah will pulverize and destroy the enemies of your job, the enemies in your home, mind, and health.

When Judah goes first, praise goes first.

We develop a relationship with Judah. It must go to a different level. It cannot stay the same. We will not do the things we used to do. We will not walk the same; we will not talk or live the same. Our eyes will become open. We will see things differently through the eyes of Judah.

We must reach beyond sharing the goodness of God with our fellow brothers and sisters in Christ. They already know we must now let Judah go first and share him with those that do not know of him. We must praise Judah. We must encourage, strengthen, and hold our brothers and sisters up in prayer and unite to become our brother's keeper.

Judah must go first!

References

Butler, Trent C. *Holman Illustrated Bible Dictionary*. Nashville, TN: Holman Bible Publishers, 2003.

Foster, Richard J. and J. B. Smith. *Devotional Classics: Selected Readings for Individuals and Groups.* New York, NY: HarperOne, 2005.

Foster, Richard J. *Streams of Living Water.* New York, NY: HarperCollins, 1998.

NIV Study Bible. Grand Rapids, MI: Zondervan, 2011.

Packer, J. I. *Knowing God.* Downers Grove, IL: InterVarsity Press, 1973.

Thomas, Gary L. *Sacred Pathways: Discover Your Soul's Path to God.* Grand Rapids, MI: Zondervan, 2010.

Thompson, Frank Charles D. D., PH.D. *Thompson Chain Reference Bible.* Indianapolis, IN: B. B., Kirkbride Bible Co., Inc., 1988.

Whitney, Donald S. *Spiritual Disciplines for the Christian Life.* Colorado Springs, CO: Navpress, 2014.

Printed in the USA
By KAE DJ Publishing
& Production